Against Certainty

Poems

SCOTT CAIRNS

SLANT
BOOKS

AGAINST CERTAINTY
Poems

First edition

Cairns, Scott
Against Certainty / by Scott Cairns -- 1st ed.

ISBN 978-1-63982-233-1 (hardcover)
ISBN 978-1-63982-232-4 (paperback)
ISBN 978-1-63982-234-8 (ebook)

Library of Congress Control Number: 2026942130

Slant Books
P.O. Box 60295
Seattle, WA 98160

www.slantbooks.org

Against Certainty

Contents

Just as an Archaeologist. . . . | 2

I. A Late Ambivalence
Instrumental Music | 5
The Demands of Appearances | 6
The Lyric Subject | 7
A Mystical Poetics | 8
My Cave | 9
What One Might Make of Visions | 10
Chemo with Coleridge | 11
Wellbeing and Woe | 12
Parable of the Interior | 13
The Storm, the Stranger's Voice, the Saint | 14
The Chapel of the Prophet Elissaíos | 15
Not So Much *Questions of Travel* | 16
Also Not Written | 18
What the God Did Not Do | 19
Against Certainty | 20
A Late Ambivalence Mid-Lent | 21
The Efficacy of Prayer | 22
Barren Prayer | 23
An Indispensable Humility | 24

II. Aphorisms At the Edge
Another Idiot Psalm | 27
Further Correspondence | 28
Confluence and Coinherence | 29
Yet One Clearing | 30
A Question | 31

Impractical Beauty | 32
Remind Me | 33
New Year | 34
Creatures of Resentment | 35
Backward Christian Soldiers | 37
Yea, the Lord Himself | 38
Bonhoeffer in Harlem | 39
As Liberations Go | 40
Abysmal Fullness | 41
What the Darkness Sometimes Serves | 44
Let Us Change | 45
Aphorisms at the Edge | 46
Modest Apocalypse | 47

III. Xarmolypi
Venetian Vespers | 53
The *Rebétis* [*Ο Ρεμπέτης*] | 55
It Remains Forbidden | 56
As I Was Saying, as I Have Said, | 57
Xarmolýpi [Χαρμολύπη] | 58
The Past, Its Presence, Prelude to a Prayer | 59
Creation without Conclusion | 61
To *Thánatos*, His Angel | 62
Lenten Metanoia | 63
Wherever the Just Exchange Their Messages | 65
What Comes Next | 66
Bright Monday Biopsy | 67
My Poor Prayer | 68
Thine Own of Thine Own | 69
Saint Simon's Cave | 70
Metakósmos [Μετακόσμος] | 71
These Few Awaiting Rescue | 72
Your *Nous*, Your Portal | 73
Makários [Μακάριος] | 74

Acknowledgments | 75

For Annie Dillard, who first opened my eyes to the beauty of not knowing, the beauty of suspecting, the joy of supposing what exceeds us.

JUST AS AN ARCHAEOLOGIST. . . .

After Auden

Nor have *I* much to say that I can prove,
But find, in saying, much that I can love.

The very words I utter have a way
To implicate a glimpse of what to say.

As I speak and listen, I hear a trace
Of provocation, this opening space

Into which the noetic font might pour
Its living waters, yielding something more.

For all I know, the Word Himself provides
Each word with lit, regenerative life,

As each is set upon the trembling page,
As each stands open there upon the stage.

The midden of each text will likely yield
Artifacts raised from their semantic field.

Words written—if they are to serve—must be
Unearthed by persons delving as they read.

I

A Late Ambivalence

INSTRUMENTAL MUSIC

Open and indeterminate, the song
        begins—just as any poem must begin—

with but one note placed upon the clear pool
        of silence—just so, and just here, upon

the sheen of its calm surface. As the poem
        resists its being pared down to narrow

denotations' glib constraints, so the sound
        of our instrumental music opens

a late path the ear is pleased to follow,
        the mind is suddenly pleased to regard,

listening to hear what might lie ahead.

        One witnesses the passage, and then makes
a momentary something of this gift

        —a sudden, surprising apprehension.
The page, the pool, the cool expanse of all

        that lay in one such space untroubled, yet
reaching beyond the pale, resists any

        closure of any term's being reduced
to *meaning made*, insists that meaning be

        made anew, forever provisional.

THE DEMANDS OF APPEARANCES

Have a look! All appearances insist
upon one's making something *of* them, one's

making something new *with* them in that broad
drama comprising the mind's persistent

colloquy—its unceasing yammering—
to find, in all that it observes, a nudge,

a compulsion to keep the ball rolling.
Cognizant or not of its obdurate

re-tooling of the thick matter at hand,
the mind makes ever more than it receives,

or the mind colors every apparent
scene with its own muddled pigments lifted

from its yet roiling, discursive palette.

THE LYRIC SUBJECT

Not *I* exactly, but surely
    a familiar confusion of

dispositions yielding with each
    new breath a voice I recognize

as offering considered speech,
    considered speech of this my own

lately rummaging mind, quite keen
    to make accommodation to

the discursive circles of which
    I am comprised, those confections

I have witnessed, and have become.

A MYSTICAL POETICS

The mystic makes his way most modestly,
keeping his auspicious glimpses mostly
to himself, and, even then, taking care
to honor them as glimpses merely, not
to dare believe that his suspicions prove
much beyond a gesture pointing toward
the bigger picture. The bigger picture
expands forever far, and farther yet
beyond his scope, and still, the mystic scop
finds no small pleasure in supposing what
yet lies sublimely out beyond each late,
successive pale the imagination plants.

Years back, my nascent mystic impulse proved
little but a hunch. I stood on the threshold—
the literal threshold—of my parents'
modest house gazing of a winter's night
upon a profoundly *im*modest, ice-
clear winter sky. I couldn't say just what
those dazzling heavens proclaimed, but I did
receive the music of their joy. Wakened
by their obscure proclamation, I said
aloud in answer *I love life*—a child's
naïve sentiment sent out into a cold
and dark surround. I recall a subtly
registered, reciprocal response—from where?
Within? Out there? Or both? I might now say
that something of a harmonic concurrence
filled the night, filled me. Since then, the limen
has continued to appear as a thin
and permeable membrane for the mind's
noetic reach, the heart's voracious wish.

MY CAVE

> *Imagine people living in a cave deep underground. The cavern has a mouth that opens to the light above, and a passage exists from this light all the way down to the people.*
>
> —Plato, *Republic*

Despite appearances, my dwelling place
        has long remained interred within the dim
hollow of my head, wherein my wits have
        proven also dim, reduced unto this
steadfast state of idiocy made plain—
        at least to me—each time I raise my eyes
to witness traces of a great expanse
        extending far beyond my hindered ken.

That is to say that, even from this dark
        corral, I glimpse amazing silhouettes
playing their elations out before me
        quickening these dead stone walls comprising
my surround. It is enough to suggest
        a life outside my head. I have witnessed
on rare occasions cast upon the rough
        sepulchral wall before me shadows live
and moving in shapes I cannot reckon.

If I could find a way to turn my head,
        and find myself thereafter disinterred,
I would do my best to venture wholly
        out to that far more spacious, endless—that
capacious realm I so far just suppose.

WHAT ONE MIGHT MAKE OF VISIONS

When first I learned that I might soon
    join the ranks of the departed,
        I was surprised by the odd thought
that if this departure were yet
    to happen, it would prove to be
        my migration from a puzzled
minority view to that more
    expansive apprehension held
        by our disabused majority
who dwell well outside the meager
    glitch of time and its narrowing
        perspective, long fraught with error.

As a boy, I once trekked a trail
    behind my father, who promised
        an alpine meadow where we would
make camp, warm our stew, and witness
    that night the heavens opening.
        They opened, opened in a way
that I could not have imagined.
    All of this is to say my dad
        made good on his promise, and I
learned then to trust even his most
    extravagant assurances.
        I now suppose that my odd, late
thought transposing my imminent
    demise into the promise of
        a better view is largely due
to what my father promised me
    as he walked that mountain trail
        some several steps before me.

CHEMO WITH COLERIDGE

The port implanted in my chest will serve
        to deliver directly to my heart
the *pharmakon* my doctor has alleged

might just give my malicious blood a nudge
        in the general direction of its
atonement, my repair. May it be blessed.

To keep my mind otherwise engaged, I
        have brought my longtime correspondent,
Mr. Coleridge, his collected works.

His collected works *are* working their charms
        to the degree that hours pass without my
dwelling on the manifestly dire straits

of those who sit adjacent, receiving
        their own, special mix of remedial
poisons. Thank you, dear Mr. Coleridge;

so long as I do not dwell overmuch
        on their gaunt and sallow visages, my own
languishing is less likely to drag me

to grim self-pity, which seems far too near
        to death. My poring over these beloved,
demanding poems infuses my anxious

heart with a balm concocted in concert
        and correspondence with the terms I hold
in hand. As I read, I say the words, each

syllable, within my mind—my very *nous*.
        I say the words there, listening, that I
might revive their symphony within me,

that from this ice I might yet build a dome.

WELLBEING AND WOE

He did not say "You shall not be tormented, you shall not be troubled, you shall not be grieved," but he said, "You shall not be overcome."

—Julian, *Revelations of Divine Love*, Chapter 68

That all shall be well I have no doubt. Still,
those meanest moments of the interim—
the *mean*time—demand interrogation.

Those meanest moments oblige our poring
over the terms expressed by certain peers
whose faith has apparently become more

a matter of negotiation, or
something like their purchasing insurance
against their ever suffering. Such terms

aver a silly supposition that
those suffering must have erred, must have sinned,
and so have earned a measure of *karmic*

pain, or retribution, or personal
comeuppance. I'm thinking how the sinless
Christ—in one meanest moment—acquiesced

to suffering, how even as he prayed
the cup might be set aside he also prayed
his own dear, acquiescing *Let it be*.

He did not offer us a path apart
from suffering, but made of his agony
a path that would allow our passing through our own.

PARABLE OF THE INTERIOR

We are driving to the interior

—Elizabeth Bishop

Every descent is difficult, but this
late, chastening trek—my puzzled mind now
dipping into an alleged cove biding
just here at the pulsing base of my throat—
proves far too much for me to undertake
on my own.
I've made this journey two times
prior, but those visits were brief—too brief—
and they had come about without my so
much as thinking I might thus descend. No,
each of those dear descents happened just as
I pored over some words I shaped without
Speaking them.
On the Holy Mountain once
the gentle Father Palamás paused mid-
prayer to raise his stole from my bowed head
to meet my eyes and say *It is not you*
who prays. When you descend into your heart,
you will find Him there, already praying.
I had no idea, then, what he meant,
but loved the notion that my heart contained
an interior more spacious than its grip.
Generally speaking, implicative
lacunae—discrete bowers opening
to reveal yet a glimpse of endlessness—
are my longtime jam.
Descent? Ascent? Who
would dare say? The interior, noetic
cove ever opens to uncharted seas.
Forever.
Still, of late, my several
earnest questions of travel have dwindled
to but one: am I able to set out?

THE STORM, THE STRANGER'S VOICE, THE SAINT

Μόνη Ξενοφῶντος

The roar of wind is what wakes me so suddenly
within the black-dark cell where I lie, the bare cell
to which the monk had led me for my late visit
to this ancient enclave on the Holy Mountain.

The roar is like no wind I've ever heard, no voice
I have ever heard the wind produce—very like
a howl followed by a moan, repeating. Awake,
I also hear rain smack hard against the window

near my head, threatening to come inside. Inside
the churning blackness into which I peer I find
black waters roiling, and out the window also
Aegean waters whipped beneath a black sky marked

by flashing lights. The moon laves the black sea with lit,
streaming lines, lavishing the froth just now aglow.

THE CHAPEL OF THE PROPHET ELISSAÍOS

Άγιος Ελισσαίος

In this close space, amid the icons and the scent
of cypresses, our Papadiamándis raised
his voice in praise to sweeten our *esperinós*.

Our *psálti*, and our dear *kosmokalógeros*
the modest, wise Aléxandros has set aside
all other matters, offering the evening prayer.

From there, he soon will wend his way up *Athinás*,
wind leftward up the cobbled hill to *Plateía*
Dexamení to meet his friends for cigarettes.

I make my own slow pilgrimage to *Ágios*
Elissaíos, and also to *Dexamení*
whenever I am once more alone in Athens.

The vespers service remains a sweet respite from
the world. As I am no *kosmokalógeros,*
I find I need such respite on the regular.

My trek from *Pláka* to my friends in *Kolonáki*
will serve to let those prayers descend to where I hold
such prayers. My late ascent to sweet *Dexamení*

will supply a modest taste of resurrection.

NOT SO MUCH *QUESTIONS OF TRAVEL*

Is it lack of imagination that makes us come
to imagined places, not just stay at home?
—Elizabeth Bishop

I don't suppose my questions are so much
questions of travel, *per se*, as they are

questions of how best to employ one's mind,
how best to use one's legs, how to manage

this fraught relationship—the so often
dismissed bond between the *fixing to go*

and the *up and going*. Speaking only
for myself, I am generally pleased

by both the fixing and the going. Plus,
I enjoy the actual transit to

and fro—as one finds in the very midst
of all travel so much to taste and see.

Each flight, road trip, and voyage during which
the mind by turns rushes ahead, by turns

hunkers and bides, is really something! Yes,
something of a roiling sea, the mind flits

and seizes, spins, reaches far as it might
ahead, which, of course, will not preclude its

intermittent reaching back as well. Still,
the best moments really have to be those

when the mind suddenly quiets, the legs
forego further ambulation, and one's

eyes more clearly fix upon the persons,
places, and things comprising one's *topos*.

Forever fogged by blithe, mediating
agency of one or another sort,

one is hard-pressed to gather much *sans* skew,
much that's true and free of obfuscation.

My questions pretty much revolve around
the most efficacious balance of my

late—and somewhat waning—hoard of psychic
and somatic energies. Should I stay?

Go? Would my laying my worn body out
upon the Aegean prove more sweetly

satisfying than my simply staying
put in the imagination's inland

dwelling? Well, yes, there, afloat and soaking,
I would still have a chance to think things over,

time and passable space to consider
all manner of pairing and repairing,

in warm and brilliant collaboration.

ALSO NOT WRITTEN

The future, for one, the future is not
yet written—dependent, as the future
must needs be, upon what each of us must

needs construct from the dense, messy midden
we observe as the present. The present
bides as our sole done deal, which even so

sits waiting to observe what each of us
will make of it. As any clear-eyed, wise
constituent cannot but grant, the God

has not composed for us a script to be
recited, no such script to be performed,
nor has the God reduced our belovéd

persons to the state of animated
puppets.
              I'd often felt chagrined in church—

the church of my youth—as some or other
yahoo at the pulpit spouted nonsense
about how God's allegéd plan for us

lay stretching out before us, awaiting
our lock-step march into its frozen tomb.
Thank God such bullshit doesn't fly. Thank God

the God's adoration for all things made
has not concluded, nor will conclude. There,
one step just past the present, some new thing

may yet be shaped, and by the hands His hand hath made.

WHAT THE GOD DID NOT DO

. . . Well, a good many of those rash things foolishly
ascribed to him. For instance, I'm convinced that he
did not *take* your son or daughter, that he did not
cause the accident, bring the dire illness, nor send
the bullet on its brutal way. God did not kill
your mom, your dad, nor take your wife *before her time*.
God did not set a time.
Evil is ubiquitous,
arrives unsent, at least unsent by God. I dare
say that I am more to blame for local evil
than is the God; I daresay that I am not more
culpable than you. I'm guessing we'd all do well
to give our best attention to one thing the God
did do, his having set you here to taste and see,
his having set you here to shape now what will be.

AGAINST CERTAINTY

Knowledge may have its purposes, but guessing
is always more fun than knowing.

—Auden, from "Archaeology"

Yes, the jig is up; no one is getting
anywhere worthwhile

so long as one demands to know just what
—precisely—obtains.

Each might, of course, suppose some small progress
toward the lit hope

of greater apprehension, of greater
gnosis, but such hope

is dashed in the moment one's conclusions
glibly shut the door.

Guessing, on the other hand, is far more
likely to move one's

poor mind somewhat nearer to a very
dear, elusive truth.

Guessing also delivers to the one
who guesses a more

efficacious modesty regarding
what dear images

the imagination thereafter limns
upon the dear, lit

page, or projects upon the ever bright
and animate air.

A LATE AMBIVALENCE MID-LENT

I am increasingly ambivalent
        regarding the efficacy
of prayer, of prayer as petition,
        ambivalent regarding any
expectation of much beyond the sweet
        balm that saying the Name avails.

The calm I know each time that I descend
        into prayer is palpable,
sufficient, also wholly sufficient
        is that stillness I suspect when—
in saying the prayer—I find myself
        descending more deeply into
whatever it is I sense descending
        into *me*, filling me even
as I speak the Name into the darkness.
        I am becoming, just the same,
aware that none of those things for which I
        ever asked—over a lifetime
of what was relatively earnest prayer—
        have altered fraught appearances
one whit. Such awareness has now led me
        to suppose that petitions remain
far from the heart of prayer, and that prayer
        is for the most part simply one's
entrance into the efficacious place
        where petition, whim, desire are eclipsed.

THE EFFICACY OF PRAYER

So, no, I won't say that prayer proves
to be all that effectual,
nor often serves to mitigate
the stinging entropy of our
aching and puzzling days, *per se*.

I speak only of my own, moot
and tepid prayer, the effects
of which are too subtle to show
here on my poor radar beyond
the random, brief, and fading blip.

My dim screen remains without doubt
compromised by a sore-gritty
accretion for which I have only
myself to blame. Even so, I
do pray, but have become less fixed

on seeing what might come of it,
having become more profoundly
aware of a quieting, what
one might apprehend as a faint,
barely tasted sweetness received

as I sink into the stillness
that prayer—and only prayer—
occasions just here, here, where my
mostly anxious heart onetime let
a sudden pulsing calm overwhelm me.

BARREN PRAYER

Our shy *Monk of the Eastern Church*,
the modest Father Lev Gillet,
has written that my apparently
barren prayer, this *prayer of the plain*
and naked will—the only prayer
of which I have what I would call
intimate knowledge—may yet prove
to be somewhat more pleasing to
the invisible and mostly
*un*apparent God than any
utterance flowing from the rare
superabundance of giddy
joy that I have too rarely known.
He avers that this is so, given
that such prayer is pure from the common,
selfish quest for spiritual delight.

I pray that he is not mistaken.
I pray that he has found for me
a sorely needed consolation.

AN INDISPENSABLE HUMILITY

Yes, you're right to suppose that every
reading of every text must be duly
approached as a fresh negotiation

Notice how the golden sun now rising
from the east illumines, gilds the western

yielding but one possible parsing of
inevitable densities lately
interrogated by a laboring

range spread out before us, reflecting there
both the sun's golden light and also all

reader discussing the matter just now
with the page, the author proving to be
unavailable—not that the author

that you've brought to this morning's crisp meeting,
nearly all you have carried—so far as

would be of much use in any case. No,
neither party is in position
ever to eclipse with narrow intentions

you can say—from your every previous
waking, every prior apprehension,

the brilliant opacities gleaming
on the page, living words swimming upon
the surface of a very great abyss.

both the conscious and the not-so-much.
Yes, I love how the light out there *mingles*
so deliciously with the light in here.

II

Aphorisms at the Edge

ANOTHER IDIOT PSALM

The Lord always hears. Of course, the Lord hears
whenever you speak to Him, and frankly
whenever you don't. Should you feel you must
from Him receive an answer, all you need
do is to open your mouth, open your mouth
and speak. Lord, to you do I speak that I
may hope to hear your inobtrusive word.

Within the shadow, within the very
shadow of death, the valley deepens, yes,
the valley looms deep, exceedingly deep,
and the descent exceedingly steep, tough
on the knees. What might one see descending
farther into the valley of death's shadow?
I observed a curious glimmer there,

as if beyond the ridge on either side
the sunlight continued bathing the late
surround in reliable radiance.
I also observed the salutary
effect its glimmer had upon my own
sentience as I beheld a great depth,
whose obscure, obscuring trail beckoned me.

FURTHER CORRESPONDENCE

After Τζένη Μαστοράκη

The deep? Yes, the deep has been
a long preoccupation
of my own as well, probably
since childhood when I first
happened upon that darkness
dwelling upon its face,
and the Spirit of God moving
upon the appalling surface
of the waters. The deep, those waters,
darkness and the Spirit both
brooding and moving upon
their surfaces have long drawn me.
My young mind then and my feeble
mind now have often borne
a measure of dizziness as my vision
plunged beyond the roiling
gesture of the deep.
And now, I'd say that I glimpse
something of the glistening deep's
extravagant reach. I suspect
that the deep extends both
up and down, extends
in every conceivable path spanning
every conceivable direction.

O dear obscure darkness, O radiant
and expansive deep, O
vertiginous, capacious waters,
receive me as into thy harbor,
thy unceasing embrace.

CONFLUENCE AND COINHERENCE

Amid the grit and raw particulate
        dimming further yet
our sore and sorely muddled wits, we pore
        above the glib constituents

of this our somewhat scattered, somewhat cracked
        kósmos, we lift
our eyes, lift up our hearts to glimpse our sad
        elements coming at long last

together again—all eroded things
        finding in the dear
Indivisible One their suspected,
        long-desired home, the confluence

of every meandering stream at last
        coinhering there
drawn within an ever-present current
        flowing from an extravagant font,

waters from which all, even now, might drink.

YET ONE CLEARING

I think that you are right to wonder why
        the view from where you sit
is so often made obscure by the odd,

exhaust- and coal-laced chiaroscuro
        now darkening nearly
every prospect, every aspect save those

clear, interior vistas one beholds
        in the very midst of
one's slow noetic descent, seeking yet

to bind one's wits with one's unspeakable
        longing, deepest desire.
Stillness has afforded yet one clearing

in which I might briefly behold something
        of what I have long sought.
Thought—as you must know—is overrated,

often ill-informed and sore misleading.
        Of late, I've given up
on thought, preferring to still my wits,

preferring to sink those wits within such
        still waters as I have
lately found to be my sole, trustworthy light.

A QUESTION

For Marcia Vanderlip

Were we unwise—here in the midst of our
        respective dotages—to adopt these,
our sixth and seventh Labradors? Most days,
        I would answer no. Our lives together
have been blessed, for thirty-plus years, with one
        or two or three sweet Labradors sharing
our bed at night, cheering our luminous
        days. When our sweet and goofy Moses passed
but four months after our sweet and patient
        Sophia, I'd thought I could not bear such
heartbreak another time. I still think that.

Wisdom proves to be a mostly subtle
        quality—one we rarely recognize
at once. It seems to slowly show itself,
        for the most part in retrospect. These dogs
will surely break our hearts, but that will be
        because they first so opened them that we
could complete our journeys yet gently attended.

IMPRACTICAL BEAUTY

Of a common winter afternoon, wet and gray
along what we have come to call our Salish Sea,
I am languishing on a comfy couch with my
dear silver Labrador, Zoey, whose fur must be

the softest fur my hand has ever touched. Her ear
must be the softest ear. And at its corner, here,

a most unnecessary and most beautiful
fold of, yes, the softest fur. Superfluities
as these puzzle the mind and make all the more full
the already overgushing heart. Gifts as these

prove inexplicable consolation to me
as I fail naming the gifts of this, our Salish Sea.

REMIND ME

Over the eastern ridge, over the yet
white peaks adjacent to our immodest
Tahoma, dawn's first amber laves the sky,
reminding our habitual darkness
of an approaching light. I would be thus
reminded, would welcome having my mind
restored to my drowsy constituents.
Yes, above that far ridge the sky receives
the dawn's amber arms, and for now I am
pleased to be somewhat restored, reminded.

NEW YEAR

Yes, our now-concluded year was largely
disappointing, and yes, of late, I find
the art of expectation for my own
improvement has become an art for which
I am not adequately skilled. The grim
electorate's *modus operandi*
appears to be ill will. Still, my feeble
sense of our collective history hints
that this trait is no late innovation.

The challenge has long been to still the heart,
to find within the *nous* a protective
cove from which one might wield a circumspect,
protective *apatheia*. The challenge
still includes our doing so without our
also being judge-y. As I say, my
expectations would suggest the new year
will likely creep along much the same as
all years past—a demanding, sticky mix
of progress and impediment, of steps
ahead and discouraging retreats. Each
is surely to be made less onerous
by the soul's firm willingness to commune
with other souls as every year proceeds
apace, pairing horrors and elations.

CREATURES OF RESENTMENT

Regarding the countless Anti-Christs

Who can say what sad mix
        of resentments has shaped
the psyches (the very
        souls) of these our boorish
brethren whose curious
        readings of the sacred
texts avail naught but self-
        assurance and dim rage.
And notice! They also
        have developed a grim,
patently satanic
        taste for absolving their
failures by impugning
        others. Who can say what
species of ignorance
        has led to this, has led
to them, and has also
        borne their astonishing
number? Is it simple
        ignorance? A chronic
forgetfulness? Dim wits?
        I dare say it was no
device occasioned by
        the God, whose signature,
longsuffering mercy
        has not yet made a blip
on their failing radars
        nor in their crusty hearts.
Sure, the Lord himself is
        alleged to have spoken
a little harshly to
        certain persons—the blithe
money changers soiling
        the Lord's temple, and those

who would wound the young—harsh,
        if understandable.
Generally speaking,
        even so, by word, by
deed, and by his famous
        disposition, the Lord's
forbearance has forborne
        the vast majority
of my sins, your sins, those
        of the resentful schmucks
indicated above.
        I don't know what to make
of them, nor have a clue
        regarding a likely
response or late recourse.
        Resentment manifests
failure of a kindred
        spirit, which spirit proves
the sole acceptable
        genius for responding
to such fraught occasions
        as these we suffer now.

BACKWARD CHRISTIAN SOLDIERS

More nearly a cranky essay than a poem

A boy among the heretics, I was obliged to sing
no few specious verses spouting vastly bad theology.

With no true ear and not much sense, our hymnists packed immodest
lines with dearly wrought embarrassments, each one wreathed by a rash

of wretched rhyme and sorely tortured rhythm. One such excess,
Onward Christian Soldiers, bore especially untoward figures,

uneasy images owing more to our predecessors'
historical blunders than they did to the Holy One Whom

we were incorrectly certain that we served. *Levitical*
seems a truer self-descriptor than is *Evangelical*

in terms of these, my people's, local disposition. I'd say
that in the interim, my heretics have not improved, not

their hymnody, nor odd theology. No, their selective
readings of the sacred texts have all but effaced the very

Face—the dear Image of *Philanthropos*—from all that passes
for thought regarding belovéd matter at hand, which matter

nonetheless continues to extend far beyond their paltry
apologia horribly pared and blithely spread to serve

as swill for the heretics' right ravenous ingestion, while—
all the while—the soul-numbing choruses continue to swell

in large and dulling measures scored to keep the infernal, not-
so-Christian troops marching to a cadence called by the one they

truly serve, that famous, fallen messenger whose yearning they
unthinking love to press into a chorus, love to sing.

YEA, THE LORD HIMSELF

One who has acquired inward possession
of God's dear commandments sees
the Lord Himself biding within them.

—Saint Isaak the Syrian

Finally, I see their real purpose—these
long-repeated admonitions dogging
our dim generations. They are laws, sure
enough, but they are more truly dear
attributes of the dear *Theánthropos*
the one God who onetime shared with Moses
some glimpse of the redemptive scheme. The Lord
will not be strange to us. The Lord will not
do or say anything in vain. He is
sure to keep the Sabbath and to keep all
days holy. He honors—now and ever—
all mothers, all fathers. He does not kill.
He is chaste in every word and deed.
The Lord takes nothing that is not His own.
His every word is true. He will not
take your belovéd, nor that of your neighbor,
nor anything that is your neighbor's. These laws
rise beyond good advice; these laws open
as revelations of the One who loves.

BONHOEFFER IN HARLEM

His buttocks going numb upon the hard
bench along the back wall of the Harlem
Abyssinian Baptist Church, the young
man has here found a way to move his love
from his head to his heart and, thereafter,
to his hands. No, he doesn't quite forget
his odd parsings of God-talk—yammerings
he has for so long considered to be
his theology—but as he visits
the hungry, poor, the deeply sad members
of the Body, he finds that it is his
own body that is most useful, is most
needed in right service to the God, whose
face he is now able to recognize
in every face his eyes reach out to touch.

AS LIBERATIONS GO

Longtime fan of liberation, *per se*,
I'm thinking lately that liberation
from the isolated self is surely
the one freedom that might finally prove
satisfying to the captive. And yes,
I remain a genuine fan of all

emancipations, have always been. Still,
the isolated self—grimmest aspect
of the self, long undeterred by any
but its own incessant need—has proven
through anxious centuries to be a most
demanding master, least munificent.

Nevertheless, freedom's lavish font bides
at each body's *noetic* center, just
beneath the heart—where the isolated
self might yet come upon pure, sweet waters
whose influence could freshen the countless
tributaries connecting us to all

other selves, and yet more perceptibly
to the very God. That same *nous* bears sole
access to the unity of persons
that we speak of when we say *The Body*,
when we glimpse how liberation from long,
fruitless isolation will require first

my opening my deepest self to those
waters whose influx will surely fill me,
loose me from isolation's abject drought.

ABYSMAL FULLNESS

Salonika

Amid the familiar, ubiquitous
wafts of cigarette smoke, amid the din
and incessant clamor of beggars' hands
rattling their few coins in their paper cups,
amid high *Romani* voices lifted
in lament—all of this amid the thick
scents of fish, of spice, coffee, and chilled blood
like a cloud pressing damp upon our rough
agorá—I learned in Salonika
finally to still my heart, even as
my eyes kept watch for any niche, or void
or cavity, any darkened, narrow
passage, dank alcove, or odd shelf where, say,
an icon may once have stood whispering
its witness.
Yes, I learned in that city
always to expect something might be found
in even the least of these—say, one, dim,
amber pool of beeswax hardened with its
one, dry, black wick bent over, or the faint
cloud of incense lingering, or a neat
midden of cigarette butts where a man
had stood deciding what to make of his
pain, or the odd coin, or the hidden door.

City of Saints, City of Ghosts, onetime
city in which peoples of all faiths shared
many astonishing centuries, lived
in concert, adjacent, enjoying each
other's habitual jokes, savory
lamb—my adopted city remains packed
with antiquity's debris and gritty
memories. On a good day you might still
count on a crumb of hospitality,
so long as you don't actually need it.

Stepping from my late train, I met again
the sense, vertiginous, that I was yet
setting foot upon a silent, crushed city
laid out like a shroud over the vast dust
and bone and rubble of several deeper
strata of loss. By now, I've developed
a keen taste for both the vertiginous
and for glimpsing the near-invisible
movement that forever fills the air, fills
my throat, fills me.
                                        Yes, every patent thing—
regardless of its place on our spectrum
of sentience—hints that it is somehow
animate, however slowly it might
move as we plod here adjacent to it.

Heartbroken, nearly fifty years ago,
I first apprehended the abyss. I
should say that it struck me differently then.
Heartbroken, I felt it as expansive
emptiness—my having, I now suppose,
projected my own bleak emptiness *then*
upon the *kósmos*. Some fifty years hence,
while the abyss is no less abysmal,
it now proves to be abysmally full,
and whatever emptiness I manage
is but remedial, salutary
and meet, allowing me these days to meet
that fullness with something like a welcome,
an embrace.
                                In the wake of his vision,
Saint Paul wrote of that fullness as very
like a sea *in which we live, move, and have
our being*. Ezekiel beheld its
movement *as a wheel within a wheel whose
rims appeared as a splay of eyes*. So, yes,
every glimpse of the abysmal fullness
sends the mind spinning, and so might witness
the mind's echoing—however it might—

that roiling energy promising ever
to exceed whatever attempts one might
make with his moot hope, his wish to name it.

WHAT THE DARKNESS SOMETIMES SERVES

Waking in my dark room, I recognize
new movement in the air above me, odd
and roiling patterns hovering just there
in the air above me. I have grown used
to this midnight waking, and fairly used
to this pairing of the caliginous
air with the vertiginous, answering
sense with which, waking thus, my soul responds.

Waking many years ago in the dense
thickness of our rainforest, I rolled out
from my dark tent to step into the night
so as to savor that depth of stillness
our rainforest uniquely held for me.
Within that stillness, I witnessed a late,
answering stillness pressing low beneath
my heart; I heard a voice there murmuring.

Tonight, similarly waking, I hear
a similar murmuring, voluble
if nonetheless inarticulate. What
might I make of such correspondences
troubling both this moment and that rising
memory? Darkness no longer frightens,
nor does this deep obscurity within.
Both appear now, meet, right, and welcoming.

LET US CHANGE

. . . in such a way that we may constantly
evolve towards what is better, being transformed
from glory to glory, and thus always improving
and ever becoming more perfect, and never
arriving at any limit of perfection.

—Saint Gregory of Nyssa

For now, I'd say the progress has been not so much
glory to glory as *glimpse to glimpse*. Still, each such

glimpse has served to reassure my *in*glorious
self that some transformation of my inner mess

might yet be underway, if hardly manifest,
mostly off the radar of those with no access

to my head. Incrementally—as I have said—
the progress remains solely observed here in my head,

which for all appearances makes moot whatever
progress has been made. Perfection, the saint avers,

remains a likely goal, not ever to be reached,
which is one such glimpse—vertiginous—how each

incremental shift occurring in our persons
must needs be noted as provisional, but one

late step along a path with no conclusion.

APHORISMS AT THE EDGE

The membranes of the mind prove
permeable, will not—
of their own—resist
the influx of their surround.

The influx of one's late surround
proves, also, to serve as sole
occasion by which the mind
meanders and proceeds.

As something of a drift amid
slow waters, the mind may yet
expand its flow to reach for what
then bides beyond appearances.

If all goes well, the mind proceeds
in its mystic mode suggesting
a descent, even as the mind,
thus attended, appears to rise.

One may find a calm and warm
embrace attending to the mind's
descent into the heart,
concurrent with its climb.

Woodsmoke laced
with fir and pine and cedar may
serve to cense whatever prayer
may meet the mind's descent and rise.

Attended by such woodsmoke wafting
wide and heavenward as one lifts
the cup to sip the campsite tea, one
is more likely then to taste and see.

Should you consider how you might
cross over, move yet beyond
the edge, should you think
to pack it in, pack light.

MODEST APOCALYPSE

What new words I speak
appear to arrive
obscurely as slow
dictation as from
an angel to a fool.

What words I offer
remain the barely
heard. They bear an all-
but-barely gathered
witness offering
dim terms of a fraught
dispensation. Yea.

I turned and I saw
just there before me
a familiar stretch
of rough road adorned
with much that appeared
sore unfamiliar,
resisting my too-
easily saying
what it was I saw.
I am obliged, then,
to speak around it.

The road before me
was lined with alder,
conifer, salal.
The road was graveled
by shale, granite, quartz.
The road ahead lay
hidden behind fine
mist that bore a sharp
resin scent, a more
soft scent of woodsmoke.

The far eastern ridge
wore a golden crown.

I turned and saw all
these things before me,
but what I saw there
before me was not
all that I beheld.

The heart of what lay
revealed was far more
the trembling áffect
of each image poised
before me. The heart
was my sense of each
lost forebear whose soul
yet trembled above
the road's glittering
grit, increasingly
gilded by the rays
reaching from the far
eastern ridge. That heart
proved the soundless pulse
wedding all that I
could see with all I
also then beheld
invisibly. What,
then, might one suppose
regarding this span
uniting things seen
with things unseen? What
might one make of such
superabundance
save that all last things
will open unto
further openings,
save that all new things
partake endlessly
as they move within

the ever widening,
expanding expanse?

III

Xarmolypi

VENETIAN VESPERS

After Anthony Hecht

The boatman's basso *barcarola* brings
a sudden, somewhat deeper blush upon
our evening waterway. With a roseate
glow afloat on their canal, the little boats
attend our slackened afternoon. And look
how each adjacent villa also bears
a rosy glow. For a moment, I don't
know where I am—or, briefly, I forget—
which mercy proves to be relatively
fleeting, as, in time, I find my wits and,
with them, I find my bearings bearing down.

Where did I begin? How did my late trek
commence? It must have been with my waking
late, thereafter staggering downstairs
to a nearly eucharistic *caffè*
e panino. Just so, the languishing
spirit is summoned back to life, called back
to what might pass for life, a passing life,
and quite passable should you care to know.

The boatman is patently on to me, but keeps
the pathos of his song intact, in time
with our slowly rocking progress, which may
as well become a late, dimming—one might
say an *evening*—retreat. So it may.

In my Eastern church, the vespers often
can acquire, in their language and their tone,
a keen sense of lament, an all but Lenten
sadness accompanied by a subtle,
latent joy—a modest joy attending
to the promise of our consolation
biding in the *nous,* where one might yet obtain
an uncommon calm, unassailable.

The boatman's *barcarola* acquiesces
to an unsurprising coda holding
yet some repetition of the theme. Time
itself has slowed and stilled, has filled the air
with space, with peace, a rising expectation.

THE *REBÉTIS* [*Ο ΡΕΜΠΈΤΗΣ*]

Τομπουρλίκα, 2017

His is a mournful music, true enough. The raw
song that our rough *rebétis* ever keeps foremost
within his heart has kept that heart quite sorely cleft,

even as it presses high into his throat, which is
just where—as far as I can gather—loss still proves
the central matter of each song, his every song.

With each new rasping phrase he bears that loss, his voice
extending to his every song a fresh and—shall
we say—a fine and efficacious ache as each

conceives in him fresh hurt for what is lost. He bears
his worn *bouzoúki* light within his arms, and here,
its strings entwine to plait the one bright thread—his fate.

His eyes ablaze, I'm guessing that he rends his own
heart first, then watches those who hear to see which hearts
tear next. We become adopted kin, who witness

how his deftly manic fingers swear that he yet
searches—even as he plays—for lamentation
proper to the ache, exile's one and lasting home.

Hear it? He comes upon a fitting brokenness
in the timbre of his voice, and having tasted
of that new elixir seems keen to drink his fill.

He lays aside his instrument to lift his drink.
Xorís glykániso, the *rakí* glistens, glows
within the glass. Imbibed, it warms the gut, where ache

translates to pleasure, the chief contentment and sole
consolation of the exile. His center spins,
warmed by a sweet confusion born of opposites.

IT REMAINS FORBIDDEN

After Pablo Neruda

Since that gracious Chilean first
        set down his most gracious tenets,
I fear that we have grown neglectful
        of his wisdom and our duty.

It is—now and ever after—
        forbidden to hate the hateful,
forbidden to resent those who
        wallow in their dear resentments,

forbidden ever to eclipse
        the needs of others in some bleak
grasp at self-assurance, or self-
        protection. The implication

at the heart of his every
        admonition is the wisdom
that each of us is utterly
        bound to every other, that each

suffers all others' sufferings,
        and each is blessed by every
blessing—all of them undeserved.

AS I WAS SAYING, AS I HAVE SAID,

severest pain will drop you to the floor;
and its descent may draw you farther yet,
where it reveals a neat, new aperture
your pain just now has opened in your head.

Wince all you want, but take your daily bread
as it conveys a special kind of salt,
which deeply seasons these last days with lead
that no degree of purging heat will melt.

Chin up. In time, when all the milk is spilt
and every searing pain becomes a pool,
your pain may yet avail some new thing still
—the now approaching apprehensible.

XARMOLÝPI [ΧΑΡΜΟΛΎΠΗ]

That grief mingled with the promise of joy

Our Lenten services are dark and slow,
made slower yet by our poor, precarious
prostrations, made darker by our bungling.

The grief—the many griefs?—with which my days
are lately colored have made the days ahead
appear as little more than shadows set

within a moot chiaroscuro. Thus
dimmed, the days ahead have obtained a measure
of dejection, and I see how quickly

one's most earnest prayer—one's life of prayer?—can
acquiesce, be collapsed, be dashed, become more
or less undone, for the most part gutted

by one untoward diagnosis. Frankly,
such response reveals just how illusory
one's sense of one's accomplishment has been.

In years past, I suppose that I have found
myself more or less this lost mid-Lent. Each year,
the Lenten services—dim-wittedly

endured—have had their expected, largely
salutary effect on my languishing.
By looking back, my looking now ahead

acquires the faint patina of a light
behind me offering some incentive to
proceed, a hope that joy may yet await.

THE PAST, ITS PRESENCE, PRELUDE TO A PRAYER

There I lay, floating on my back upon the blue
Aegean, that same sea pressed against the sun-bathed
sands of Serifos. I was suddenly thinking
of the past, the blurred nature of its presence, and how—

however blurred its áffect—the past presses so
aggressively against . . . is it the chest? the throat?
somewhere low in the throat? high in the chest? making
breath itself a chore, and making the mind dip yet

again into the familiar dread that rests so
like a dead, salt sea, deep in the gut. It remains
a calm sea—*σαν λάδι**, as the Greeks say—but is
no less a sea of dread. I swim there every

so often—usually when certain moments of the past
remind me of their presence, or when the present
for a moment trembles with a strange resemblance
to the past, or when thoughts of the future trouble

the surface calm, the shimmering oils of that sore
expansive sea that is the past. Yes, my modest
meditation proves to be more than a little
circular in its movement, but even that late

gesture proves emblematic of the past, partaking
of the roiling confusions found whenever thoughts
about the future move the glib clock-hands hard
to the left, into the past. If I were floating

in Australia, I'm guessing the clock-hands would spin
hard to the right. Even the sweetest of my past
moments—images of my young daughter, my young son,
my young wife—send me into new anxieties

about what is yet to come—their lives without me.
God, may my descent not leave them bereft, but pleased
to lie back upon this same cradling sea, feeling
on their faces the warmth of the Aegean sun,

trusting that I have not gone quite so far away
as in moments of our dread I may appear to be.

* *σαν λάδι—like oil*

CREATION WITHOUT CONCLUSION

Δημιουργία χωρίς τέλος

What? You had thought creation to be
 a one-time act concluded? You
were given to imagine the *kósmos*
 complete, or in any case moving
toward an eventual, conclusive end? Bummer.

In our modest beginning—wisdom
 avers—we just might witness as well
the nature of an end, an outcome;
 in our beginning, still, our end
might open unto apprehension.

The God without beginning—being
 our beginning—is surely our end,
which makes our end an endless one,
 continuing ever, just as He
continues, and we in Him continue.

Partaking of Himself, we can't help
 but become, like Him, eternal,
and endlessly more like Him, ongoing.
 Neither does this vertiginous journey
conclude, neither does it fail. Yes, proceed.

TO *THANATOS*, HIS ANGEL

Longtime acquaintance
        whom I have seldom
feared, whose visits I
        have even so found
mildly distressing,
        whose message yet hums
for the greater part
        inarticulate,
faint, if not to be
        mistaken, you whose
face gleams in my dim
        room, as shade flows more
fully into what
        remains of my day,
greetings! What news will
        you bring to me this
visit? I might still
        have a guess. Since my
grim diagnosis,
        I have awaited
your more insistent
        voice, but had not known
its music, nor thought
        that its edges would
now have softened so.

LENTEN METANOIA

After Eliot

My having lately made a likely turn,
I do not hope to turn again, nor hope
to know what I had long desired to know.

Repentance has become me, has made me
more becoming. Which is to say that I,
having turned, am hoping henceforth to be
at every step becoming. My being,
per se, has long been—if you will not mind
my saying so—a matter of sequenced
and discrete placeholders merely. I'd say
each feels to have been—so far as lasting
progress goes—a quiet disappointment.

By every indication, some years back
I came upon an efficacious path
stretching far ahead. My expectation
had me pressing on, and covering far
more ground than I have actually covered.
My place and time, at each turn, have proven
for the most part squandered, for the most part
unredeemed. The burden of my words has
weighed on me mostly as interior
perplexity. The burden of the Word—
however—bestows a more compelling
heft, has led to my desire willingly
to shed my previous adoration
of my words, my word-hoard, my singular
voice echoing my own dim wits alone.

The Word Himself, then—never to be named
conclusively—continues yet to woo
me, as that Word trembles, very nearly
as a bubbling in my waking *nous*, just
here, here, low in the throat, high in the chest.

My best guess is that we—all of us?—must
press our terms for information, must yet
pore over what utterances we shape
to catch a glimpse of what it is we have
long hoped to apprehend.

This evening,
I came upon the memory of one
particular trek on the palpably
Holy Mountain—one long day I wandered
that sweet path we call the wilderness. There,
along the way, I met no one, but felt
attended, even so. I prayed the prayer.
I prayed and walked a dappled path beneath
high-reaching oaks and pines, my one prayer
also reaching high.

Above the hidden
cove my map named *Kafsokalyvia*,
I found a bowl beneath a tree, a bowl
placed oddly near the path, set at the base
of a soaring beech. I left three fragrant
oranges, my sack of almonds, a card
bearing the image of my Saint Isaak.

I walked thereafter yet more palpably
attended. Late that evening, I passed
through the gate of Saint Anna's lovely skete.
In the courtyard, Father Cheruvim sat
smiling, waving me to a seat close by.
In English, he said that he'd been waiting.

WHEREVER THE JUST EXCHANGE THEIR MESSAGES

Homage to W.H. Auden

Wherever the blameless deign to linger—
where they pause
along their endless ascent, precisely
where they slow
their steps, stop, drop to their knees, puzzling
at their dim
complicity in what several losses
they yet sense
in their otherwise calm, unaffected
guts, just where
our blinking, exemplary forebears think
suddenly
to wait along their late, posthumous trek,
that is just
where I would ask to arrive and—if allowed—
would yet ask
a word, and would pore over their murmured
messages
for so much as a clue. Yes, that is where
I would hope
to arrive, arrive in time to hear such
messages
as those the just there whisper modestly,
each to each.
Yes, I hope there to awaken in time
to receive
what deliverance those messages bear.
Finally,
I have heard—in my own heart's pulse—the caked
debris that
has kept me, thus far, deafened by my own
impediments.

WHAT COMES NEXT

Ἐν αὐτῷ γὰρ ζῶμεν καὶ κινούμεθα καὶ ἐσμέν,
ὡς καί τινες τῶν καθ' ὑμᾶς ποιητῶν εἰρήκασι
Τοῦ γὰρ καὶ γένος ἐσμέν.

—Πράξεις 17.28

Yes, I want to be healed, but more than that
I want very much to see what comes next,
hoping that what comes next will include my
belovéd dogs—my every loving dog—
leaping once more into my arms.

Also,

my parents, my departed friends, and all
lost loved ones meeting again, gathering
there in the embrace of the One in Whom
we might continue to move, continue
to have our being, in Whom we might yet live.

BRIGHT MONDAY BIOPSY

April 21, 2025

Just yesterday, in the very early hours
of Great and Holy Pascha, I savored
the Resurrection of our murdered God.

I sang *Χριστός Ανέστη** with all my heart
at least a dozen times and shouted *Truly*
He Is Risen in a good half-dozen languages.

Arriving home at 3:00 a.m., we broke our fast
by cracking open our several scarlet eggs.
Waking late that same morning, I prepared

our customary feast—lamb on the *soúvla*,
spanakópita, the lemony Greek spuds,
the *horiatiki saláta*, the *tsatsíki*, all

such goodnesses for the family gathered
to feast, to drink the wine, to kiss one another
with eyes glistening, our hearts in our throats.

The same as every blesséd year—thank God.
Today, I have an early appointment allowing
my doctor to chisel yet another aperture

into my hip in his eagerness to confirm
that the chemotherapy has done its work,
that I am, however briefly, on the mend.

May it be blessed, as we say. May the earth's
resurrection extend its life-giving agency
to my body one more time. May my dear

belovéds find this season to be as sweet
as every other. May the world's restoration
extend to everything that breathes. *Amin.*

* *Χριστός Ανέστη—Christ is Risen*

MY POOR PRAYER

Therefore, I say to you, whatever things you ask when you pray, believe that you receive them, and you will have them.

—Mark 11:24

I don't know what one is to make
of such a thing—Christ's saying such
a thing, suggesting that one's sore
fickle belief bears agency
for altering a circumstance,
and our securing what we ask.

Given some long experience
to the contrary, I cannot
but infer the problem to be
my poor faith yielding nought but fruit-
less prayer. Peace, for instance, how long
must one pray for peace to see it?

Just last week, Father Iákovos
listened as I confessed my doubt
in prayer's serving much beyond
a warm balm for the one who prays.
He asked if I had peace as I
prayed. Well, no, peace eludes me still.

There's the problem, he said, *recall*
the first great litany—"In peace
do we pray to the Lord." In peace,
we may yet hope to pray for peace.
The toughest catch of all, I thought,
and most crippling of my failures.

I would yet say Lord, I believe.
I would say Help my unbelief.

THINE OWN OF THINE OWN

Epiphany at Saint Nicholas Church

What does one have to offer, save
what one already holds, just here.

What does one hold in hand, save that
with which one has been blessed? Witness

the young priest as he lifts the cup
and murmurs *Thine Own of Thine Own.*

Yes, I murmur with him, Thine Own
of Thine Own. As I speak, I see.

I see the boundlessness stretching
here before me—it is Thine Own.

I hope to grasp this one true thought
within my hobbled *nous*, even

as I am obliged to let go
all else, every other thing.

SAINT SIMON'S CAVE

June, 2025

I was already feeling weary, already
thinking that this might, in fact, be my last visit
to my beloved *Simonópetra*, my last
visit with my beloved Father Iákovos.

My hope for the morning was modest—I had hoped
to light a candle and say an earnest prayer
for a dear friend suffering. My hope for the day
was to find again the peace that I had found here
some twenty years before. How might I say this now?
I had hope, but had no faith.
                    My earnest prayers
over the past year had appeared to yield little,
though the act of prayer—the leaning in, the deep
calm of attending to The Presence—continued
to be a sorely needed balm, almost enough.
My morning plan proved unlikely, as the narthex
of the *katholikón* held no candle stand, nor
could I recall where such a stand stood waiting.

Dim-witted, worn and weary, I thought to find
some little peace in Saint Simon's cave some distance
up the road. Entering the cave, I cracked my head
on the low doorframe, hard enough to occasion
tears, as I clamped shut my eyes, and felt my way
to the stone bench inside. I prayed what I would call
a broken prayer—worn, weary, and suddenly
without hope or faith.
                    When I became calm enough,
I opened my eyes, and through the dim blur of tears
saw before me the single vigil lamp ablaze,
saw the grip of sweet beeswax candles awaiting me
in the holy narthex of dear Saint Simon's cave.

METAKÓSMOS [METAKÓΣMOΣ]

. . . whether in the body, I cannot tell; or whether out of the body, I cannot tell.

—2 Corinthians 12:2

Yes, here beyond the world, the air is thin,
and I too have become insubstantial—
well, *less* substantial. The body—I now
can say—is not ever fully eclipsed
by spirit, but becomes somewhat lighter,
more readily alight, by which I might
also aver both lit and luminous.

The darkness has not overcome the light.
The darkness really never stood a chance,
being, as it is, an absence, a sad
aberration, a nothing pressing hard
against a superabundant something.
As I say—as I gather in a glance—
the feeble darkness never stood a chance.

THESE FEW AWAITING RESCUE

When the building collapsed, these few
survived because, in that collapse
of concrete and steel, the fallen
structures occasioned, here and there,
a void in which each could lie, uncrushed,
awaiting rescue.
                                        And within
that void the darkness proved complete,
as well as the silence, which rang
in their ears as yet another
appalling void, still opening.

Each had already descended
farther down than any had yet
bowed into their own noetic
voids, but in that darkness and in
that murmuring stillness they found
a path to appalling strata
that for so long, unsuspected,
had been their deeper firmament.

YOUR *NOUS*, YOUR PORTAL

Yes, if ever you are lucky enough
to descend into the *nous*—that still cove
deep within your person—you will have also

successfully risen far above all things,
so far above what we have thought to call
the universe that you will find yourself

before the God, the very God, and if
you will be healed, you will need only reach
to touch the light that is His garment's hem.

MAKÁRIOS [ΜΑΚΆΡΙΟΣ]

The blesséd one

Blesséd is the one—blesséd and right full
of joy—whose eyes are not altogether
fixed upon the chafe and grit pressed upon
the heart, whose eyes see, however dimly,
just enough past the mess to grant the heart
a glimpse of joy surpassing what passes
for the big picture. The big picture's scope
proves never quite to offer what I would
call *the real deal*, the actual, lavish
glee infusing all things at base. Holy,
holy, holy, yo! And endless. And all.
All that. And ever, as I was just now saying.

Acknowledgments

Earlier iterations of the following poems have previously appeared in these publications:

Christianity and Literature
Image
Inkwell
Living City
Orthodoxy Now
Poetry International
Presence
The Schooner
Sehnsucht
Spiritus

This book was set in Garamond Premier Pro, designed by Robert Slimbach and published in 1989. It had its genesis in 1988 when Adobe senior type designer Robert Slimbach visited the Plantin-Moretus Museum in Antwerp, Belgium, to study their collection of Claude Garamond's metal punches and type designs.

This book was designed by Shannon Carter, Ian Creeger, and Gregory Wolfe. It was published in hardcover, paperback, and electronic formats by Slant Books, Seattle, Washington.

Cover image: Daniel Burka via Unsplash.

www.ingramcontent.com/pod-product-compliance
Lightning Source LLC
Chambersburg PA
CBHW030612010926
50774CB00039B/834
9781639822324